P9-DEI-760

EDGE
BOOKS

BLOODIEST BATTLES

ONE MILLION LOST

THE BATTLE OF THE SOMME

BY BARBARA DAVIS

CONSULTANT:
Tim Solie
Adjunct Professor of History
Minnesota State University, Mankato

Capstone press

Mankato, Minnesota

Edge Books are published by Capstone Press,
151 Good Counsel Drive, P.O. Box 669, Mankato, Minnesota 56002.
www.capstonepress.com

Library of Congress Cataloging-in-Publication Data
Davis, Barbara J., 1952–
    One Million Lost: the Battle of the Somme / by Barbara Davis.
    p. cm. — (Edge books. Bloodiest battles)
    Summary: "Describes events before, during, and after the Battle of the
Somme, including key players, weapons, and battle tactics." — Provided by
publisher.
    Includes bibliographical references and index.
    ISBN-13: 978-1-4296-1938-7 (hardcover)
    ISBN-10: 1-4296-1938-4 (hardcover)
    1. Somme, 1st Battle of the, France, 1916 — Juvenile literature. I. Title.
II. Title: Battle of the Somme. III. Series.
D545.S7D38 2009
940.4'272 — dc22   2008000613

Editorial Credits
Mandy Robbins, editor; Bob Lentz, designer/illustrator; Jo Miller,
    photo researcher

Photo Credits
Art Resource, N.Y./Adoc-photos, 26; Snark, 25
Getty Images Inc./Hulton Archive, cover (middle), 6, 8, 13, 15;
    Morgan-Wells, 20–21; W & D Downey, 12; Time Life Pictures/Mansell,
    16; U.S. Army Signal Corps, 29
The Image Works/Topham, cover (top, bottom), 18–19
Mary Evans Picture Library, 4

TABLE OF CONTENTS

CHAPTER 1

THE FIRST WORLD WAR

Lord Horatio Kitchener (right), British secretary of state for war, visited recruiting offices to persuade men to join the British Army.

LEARN ABOUT

> PALS BATTALIONS
> KEY PLAYERS
> ON THE FRONT LINES

In the summer of 1916, the countries of Europe were fighting World War I (1914–1918). The Battle of the Somme was meant to be a short attack on the Germans by the British and French. But it stretched into months. For weeks, smoke rolled over the battlefield. Bullets screamed through the air as young soldiers scrambled for cover. Grenades made the ground explode into fountains of mud and rocks.

Many British soldiers fought in Pals Battalions. These groups of soldiers came from the same towns or cities. The young men in these groups signed up to fight alongside their friends and neighbors. When the Battle of the Somme finally ended, many towns had lost hundreds or thousands of young men.

When Archduke Franz Ferdinand of Austria (right) was killed, his friend Kaiser Wilhelm II of Germany (left) helped launch World War I.

A Battle of Nations

The nations of Europe had been fighting over territory in Europe and other parts of the world for years. Eventually, the constant conflict exploded into World War I. It was the first war in history to involve countries from all over the world.

The war began in August 1914 when Germany invaded Belgium and France. Germany was part of a group of nations called the Central powers. The group also included Austria-Hungary and Turkey. They fought against the armies of the Allied forces, or Allies. The Allies included Great Britain, France, and the United States.

The Western Front

The Allies and the Central powers fought in Europe, Asia, and Africa. In Europe, the Germans fought the British and the French along the western front. This narrow strip of land ran from the North Sea to the border of Switzerland. The Allies stopped the Central powers' march into France along the western front.

The Central powers thought that if they took over France, they could conquer all of Europe. The Allies were determined to stop that from happening. The two sides fought battle after battle along the western front. One of the deadliest was the Battle of the Somme.

CHAPTER 2

THE BIG PUSH

Trenches were dirty, crowded, and smelly places to live.

For 18 months, fighting raged along the western front with very little success on either side. The Germans could not move any farther into France. The Allies could not push them out.

Trenches and Dugouts

Early on, German troops dug **trenches** and **dugouts** along the front lines. Trenches were usually 6 to 7 feet (1.8 to 2.1 meters) wide and 7 to 8 feet (2.1 to 2.4 meters) deep. These structures gave the Germans protection against Allied attacks.

The German defense plan was a good one. After failing to budge the Germans, the Allies built trenches too. Soon there were long lines of trenches facing each other along the western front.

trench — a long, narrow ditch
dugout — a shelter dug out of the ground

Both armies strung sharp barbed wire in front of the trenches. The wire ran in a tangled coil about 40 yards (37 meters) wide and 460 miles (740 kilometers) long.

In some places, the trenches of opposing armies were only a few miles apart. In other places, there were towns and farms between the Allies and the Germans.

> TRENCH LIFE

Life in the trenches was bearable at best and miserable at worst. Cave-ins were common. A cave-in could bury soldiers under a pile of mud. When it rained, water collected in muddy pools. Soldiers lived in the cold, wet mud for weeks.

During periods of heavy fighting, it was difficult to move out dead soldiers. Rats fed on the bodies. Lice, beetles, and other bugs picked at the living as well as the dead. The pests and filthy conditions spread horrible diseases that were as deadly to soldiers as bullets.

At the beginning of World War I, Sir Douglas Haig's military career spanned more than 30 years.

A Daring Plan

In December 1915, British Field Marshal Sir Douglas Haig and French General Joseph Joffre planned a huge joint attack. The British and French would confront the Germans near the Somme River. The Allies called the plan the "Big Push."

The Big Push was scheduled for early July 1916. The Allied forces planned to pound the Germans with every kind of firepower. They hoped this would force the Germans to retreat or give up.

General Joseph Joffre had been part of the French military for nearly 45 years when World War I broke out.

Allied Preparations

The British and French forces totaled 750,000 men. Their strategy was to attack an area about 23 miles (37 kilometers) long. The British would lead the attack on the north side of the Somme River. The French planned to support the British efforts on the south side of the river.

German Defenses

The Germans had only about 300,000 men. But they had more weapons than the Allies, including 1,000 machine guns. The Germans had also built two rows of dugouts and trenches along their lines instead of one. The Allies would have to get through both well-defended rows if they were to win.

German machine gunners often wore gas masks to protect themselves from enemies' poisonous gas attacks.

> LUXURIOUS DIGS

FACT:

Some German dugouts had electricity, fireplaces, chairs, and beds. Others had passageways that connected one dugout to another.

CHAPTER 3

A LONG AND BLOODY BATTLE

When soldiers attacked from the trenches, it was called going "over the top."

The Allies began their attack by blasting the Germans with **artillery**. They started firing shells on June 24, 1916. For seven days, about 3,000 Allied artillery guns fired more than 1.7 million shells at the Germans. The ground shook with explosions. Trees, rocks, and dirt flew high into the air. Fires blazed, and the air filled with dark smoke. Haig and the other Allied commanders were sure that the attack had weakened the German defenses.

artillery — cannons and other large guns

No Surprise

What the Allies didn't know was that the Germans had prepared
for the attack. Reports from German spy planes had alerted them of the
Allies' planned attack. Weeks before the attack, the Germans had dug even
stronger dugouts.

When the Allies' bombs hit, the German defenses were ready. Soldiers
and officers moved into the dugouts and waited out the artillery attack.

FACT

> LOCHNAGAR CRATER

The Allies' mines created Lochnagar Crater.
This large hole is 269 feet (82 meters) wide
and 70 feet (21 meters) deep.

The Germans knew that when the bombing stopped, the Allied
infantry advance would begin. The Allies would not bomb their own men.
At that time, the Germans would come out of the dugouts and fight.

infantry — soldiers trained to fight on foot

Attack!

At 7:30 in the morning on July 1, a series of explosions blasted through the air. They signaled the beginning of the Allied infantry attack. The first lines of Allied soldiers started moving toward the German lines.

The soldiers walked slowly across no-man's-land, the area between the Allied and German lines. The Allies assumed the artillery attack had weakened the Germans. They didn't think they would meet much resistance.

The Allied soldiers were confident they would beat the Germans when they attacked on July 1, 1916.

Fighting Back

In an instant, the air screamed with bullets. German machine guns mowed down the advancing Allied soldiers. The German soldiers loaded and reloaded. They fired **mortar** shells and threw hand **grenades** at the Allied soldiers. Soon, the battlefield was littered with bodies.

Small Gains

The second wave of Allied troops was more cautious. They crouched and crawled along the ground. They found cover wherever they could. Allied rifles spat bullets at the Germans. The German rifles fired back. Fighting was fierce and bloody.

Allied soldiers did manage to capture the towns of Mametz, Montauban, and Curlu. But many other towns remained under German control.

---

mortar — a short cannon that fires shells high into the air

grenade — a small bomb that can be thrown or launched

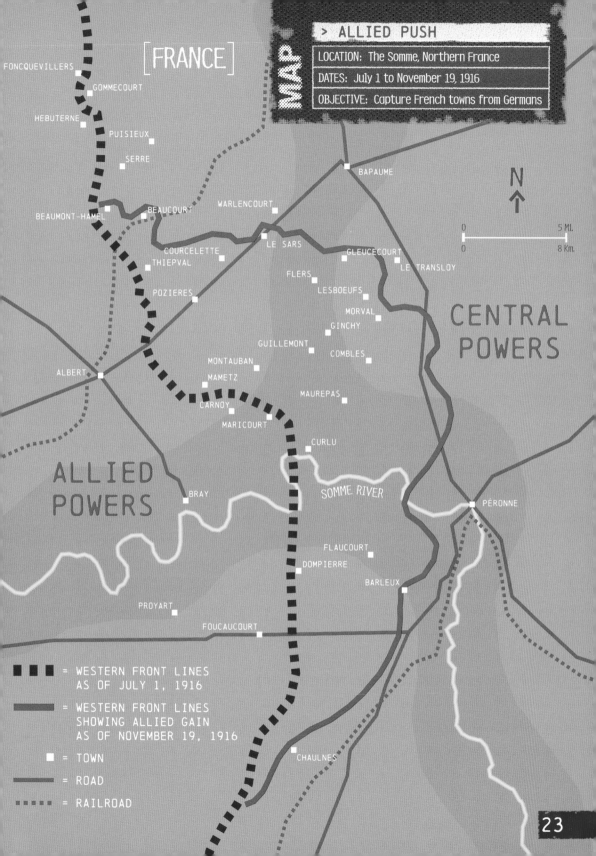

[FRANCE]

> ALLIED PUSH

LOCATION: The Somme, Northern France

DATES: July 1 to November 19, 1916

OBJECTIVE: Capture French towns from Germans

FONCQUEVILLERS

GOMMECOURT

HEBUTERNE

PUISIEUX

SERRE

BAPAUME

N

0 ———————— 5 MI.
0 ———————— 8 Km.

BEAUCOURT

WARLENCOURT

BEAUMONT-HAMEL

LE SARS

COURCELETTE

GLEUCECOURT

THIEPVAL

LE TRANSLOY

FLERS

POZIERES

LESBOEUFS

MORVAL

GINCHY

GUILLEMONT

COMBLES

MONTAUBAN

CENTRAL
POWERS

ALBERT

MAMETZ

CARNOY

MAUREPAS

MARICOURT

CURLU

ALLIED
POWERS

BRAY

SOMME RIVER

PÉRONNE

FLAUCOURT

DOMPIERRE

BARLEUX

PROYART

FOUCAUCOURT

= WESTERN FRONT LINES
   AS OF JULY 1, 1916

= WESTERN FRONT LINES
   SHOWING ALLIED GAIN
   AS OF NOVEMBER 19, 1916

■ = TOWN

= ROAD

...... = RAILROAD

CHAULNES

23

At the end of the first day of battle, the Allies had failed to sweep the Germans from the Somme. It had been a day of disaster for the British Army. The army suffered 57,470 **casualties**. In comparison, the Germans had 10,000 to 12,000 casualties. The next morning, surviving soldiers looked over a battlefield soaked in blood.

Continuing the Push

Even though their first attack had failed, the Allies attacked again the next morning. This time they changed their strategy. The Allies no longer believed that the Germans could be pushed out of the Somme in one battle. The Allies were determined to keep fighting and slowly push out the Germans. The Germans, however, were just as determined to stay. Both sides prepared for more bloodshed.

Between July 2 and November 19, 1916, the Allies led 12 more attacks. In the end, the weather put an end to the fighting. Cold weather and snow made fighting impossible.

casualty — a person who is injured, captured, killed, or missing in a war

FACT:

More British soldiers were killed during the first day of the Battle of the Somme than on any other day of the battle.

After the first day of battle, thousands of wounded soldiers waited for medical care.

CHAPTER 4

A SYMBOL OF DEATH

Many historians blame bad planning and poor strategy for the huge loss of life during the Battle of the Somme.

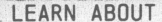
The Battle of the Somme was one of the bloodiest battles of World War I. More than 1 million British, French, and German soldiers were killed, wounded, or missing in action. The battle came to represent the horrible death and destruction of World War I. The high death toll hurt morale in Great Britain and France. No one had expected the cost in human lives to be so high.

Many people saw the Battle of the Somme as an example of poor strategy by the Allied commanders. For the horrible price in lives, the Allies advanced only about 6 miles (10 kilometers) at the widest point. The Germans did not retreat until early 1917, when they chose to move to a new line of defenses.

End of the War

World War I ended on November 11, 1918. In the end, the Allies defeated the Central powers. During World War I, soldiers came face-to-face with a new type of war. The Battle of the Somme was no exception. Modern technology made killing easier than ever before. Weapons were made by the thousands in factories, instead of being individually made by hand. Tanks and airplanes were used for the first time in battle.

The cost in lives was huge during World War I. More than 17 million people were killed or wounded. Many of these soldiers made their last stand at the Battle of the Somme.

People in Allied nations around the world celebrated the end of World War I on November 11, 1918.

GLOSSARY

Allies (AL-eyes) — a group of countries that fought together in World War I; the Allies included the United States, Great Britain, France, and Italy.

artillery (ar-TI-luhr-ee) — cannons and other large guns used during battles

casualty (KAZH-oo-uhl-tee) — someone who is injured, captured, killed, or missing in an accident, a disaster, or a war

Central powers (SEN-truhl PAU-uhrs) — countries that fought together in World War I; the Central powers included Germany, Turkey, and Austria-Hungary.

dugout (DUHG-out) — a shelter dug out of the ground or in the side of a hill

grenade (gruh-NAYD) — a small explosive device that often is thrown at enemy targets

infantry (IN-fuhn-tree) — a group of soldiers trained to fight and travel on foot

mortar (MOR-tur) — a short cannon that fires shells or rockets high in the air

trench (TRENCH) — a long, narrow ditch; soldiers in World War I fought in trenches.

READ MORE

Adams, Simon. *World War I.* DK Eyewitness Books. New York: DK, 2007.

Ross, Stewart. *The Battle of the Somme.* The World Wars. Chicago: Raintree, 2004.

Ross, Stewart. *World War I.* Timelines. North Mankato, Minn.: Arcturus, 2007.

INTERNET SITES

FactHound offers a safe, fun way to find Internet sites related to this book. All of the sites on FactHound have been researched by our staff.

Here's how:
1. Visit *www.facthound.com*
2. Choose your grade level.
3. Type in this book ID **1429619384** for age-appropriate sites. You may also browse subjects by clicking on letters, or by clicking on pictures and words.
4. Click on the **Fetch It** button.

FactHound will fetch the best sites for you!

INDEX